LILIʻUOKALANI

Ruby Hasegawa Lowe

Illustrated by
Robin Yoko Burningham

Kamehameha Schools Press
Honolulu

KAMEHAMEHA SCHOOLS

Inquiries should be addressed to:

Kamehameha Schools Press
1887 Makuakāne Street
Honolulu, Hawaiʻi 96817

The paper used in this publication
meets the minimum requirements of
American National Standard for Library Sciences—
Permanence of Paper for Printed Library Materials,
ANSI Z39.48-1992

Printed in the United States of America

ISBN 0-87336-018-4

*Cover photo courtesy of Bishop Museum
(retouched with permission)*

10 09 08 07 06   9 8 7 6 5

Dedicated

to the children

of Hawai‘i

Table of Contents

Preface

This book is one of a series originally written by faculty in a Kamehameha reading program. The books are designed to increase students' reading skills and their knowledge of Hawaiian history and culture by focusing on topics such as the Hawaiian monarchy.

Some of these books have been translated from their original English into Hawaiian through the efforts of the staff of the Kamehameha Schools Hawaiian Studies Institute.

We are pleased at the reception both the English and the Hawaiian editions have received from educational and general audiences.

Michael J. Chun, Ph.D.
President
Kamehameha Schools

Acknowledgments

Several people helped to make this book possible. I would like to thank Kaipo Hale, Hawaiian resource specialist at Kamehameha Schools; Kilolani Mitchell, a long time consultant at Kamehameha Schools and Marian Welz, retired principal of Kamehameha Schools Preparatory Department.

R.H.L.

LILI'UOKALANI

Photo by Kamehameha Schools

Introduction

Lili'uokalani, last reigning monarch of Hawai'i, did not believe in being a queen in name only. She was a determined and forthright person who believed the Hawaiian *ali'i* knew best how to rule their own people. This is the story of her life and her struggle to keep the kingdom of Hawai'i an independent nation.

Liliʻu as a baby with Keohokālole and Kapaʻakea.

Early Years

*L*ili'uokalani was born on September 2, 1838, to the **High Chief** Caesar Kapa'akea and High Chiefess Keohokālole. She was named Lili'u (Smarting) Kamaka'eha (The Sore Eye). It may seem as if the baby had an eye problem when she was born, but this was not so. The High Chiefess Kīna'u, who gave Lili'u her name, was the one with the sore eye.

Besides Lili'u Kamaka'eha, her Christian name was Lydia, a name given her at her baptism. It was not until years later that she was called Lili'uokalani.

Upon her birth Lili'u became the child of *hānai* parents, High Chief Pākī and High Chiefess Konia. *Hānai* was an old Hawaiian custom in which one family would give a child to one another. When a child was given in *hānai* to a chiefly or royal family the child gained rank from the new family. This practice helped to keep the chiefs closely bonded.

Konia, Lili'u's *hānai* mother, was the granddaughter of Kamehameha I. Konia and Pākī had a daughter of their own, Bernice Pauahi, who became Lili'u's *hānai* sister.

Lili'u was cared for by an attendant named Kaikai. Kaikai had given her children away and cared for Lili'u as her own.

School Years

At the age of four Lili'u went to the Chiefs' Children's School (later known as The Royal School). It was not an ordinary school. Students spent both days and nights there. Being quite young, Lili'u was not very happy to be away from home. When Kaikai took her to the school Lili'u cried and would not let go of Kaikai's neck. However, Lili'u had no choice in the matter and Kaikai left her there. She missed her *hānai* parents and her home and looked forward to Sundays and holidays when she could go home.

KA NONANONA.

"E ka mea hiamoe, e helo oe i ka nonanoa, e nana i kona noao a e hoonaauao iho." *Solomona.*

Buke I. HONOLULU, OAHU, IULAI 20, 1841. **Pepa 2.**

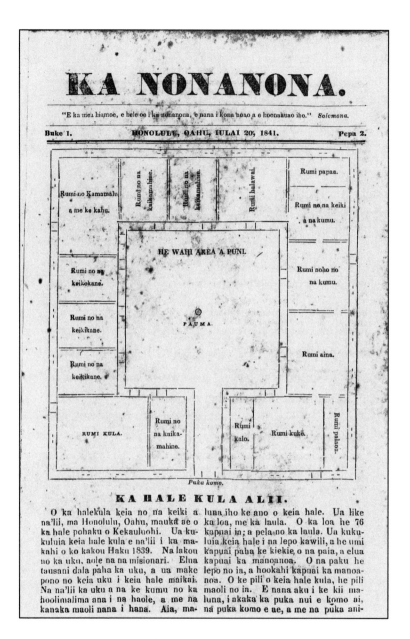

Rumi no Kamamalu a me ke kahu.

Rumi no na kaikamahine.

Rumi no na kaikamahine.

Rumi halawai.

Rumi papaa.

Rumi no na keiki a na kumu.

HE WAHI AREA A PUNI.

Rumi no na keikokane.

Rumi noho no na kumu.

Rumi no na keikikane.

PAUMA.

Rumi aina.

Rumi no na keikikane.

RUMI KULA.

Rumi no na kaikamahine.

Rumi kalo.

Rumi kuke.

Rumi paalaoi.

Puka komo.

KA HALE KULA ALII.

O ka halekula keia no na keiki a na'lii, ma Honolulu, Oahu, mauka ae o ka hale pohaku o Kekauluohi. Ua kukuluia keia hale kula e na'lii i ka makahi o ko kakou Haku 1839. Na lakou no ka uku, aole na na misionari. Elua tausani dala paha ka uku, a ua make pono no keia uku i keia hale maikai. Na na'lii ka uku a na ke kumu no ka hoolimalima ana i na haole, a me na kanaka maoli nana i hana. Aia, ma-luna iho ke ano o keia hale. Ua like ka loa, me ka laula. O ka loa he 76 kapuai in; a pela no ka laula. Ua kukuluia keia hale i na lepo kawili, a he umi kapuai paha ke kiekie, o na paia, a elua kapuai ka manoanoa. O na paku he lepo no ia, a hookahi kapuai ka manoanoa. O ke pili o keia hale kula, he pili maoli no in. E nana aku i ke kii maluna, i akaka ka puka nui e komo ai, na puka komo e ae, a me na puka ani-

Mr. and Mrs. Amos Cooke were her teachers at the school. The Cookes were missionaries from New England who had the task of teaching the children. As Liliʻu tried to adjust to the ways of the Cookes, the Cookes also attempted to understand and work with her.

·R BURNINGHAM·

Lili'u playing the piano for Pauahi.

Despite her unhappiness Lili'u did very well at the school. She studied hard and spent six hours a day on reading, writing, English grammar, arithmetic and spelling. She developed Christian beliefs which helped her throughout her life. She learned to play the piano with the help of her sister Bernice and Mrs. Cooke. Besides playing the piano, Lili'u could memorize tunes easily and sing beautifully.

Haleakalā, home of Liliʻu's hānai *family.*

When the Cookes closed the school in 1848 Lili'u was overjoyed to return to Haleakalā, the home of her *hānai* parents. She was much happier attending a day school and being tutored at home. During this time she studied Greek and developed a love for the myths and legends of ancient Greece. She could easily relate these legends to her own Hawaiian background.

Seated (from left to right), Laura Cleghorn, Princess Liliʻuokalani,
Princess Likelike and Keawepoʻole.
Standing, Thomas Cleghorn, John O. Dominis and Archibald S. Cleghorn.
Photo courtesy of Bishop Museum

Marriage

When Lili'u was twenty-four years old she married John Owen Dominis. She had known John in her youth while at the Chiefs' Children's School. The wedding was held at Haleakalā on September 16, 1862.

After their marriage Lili'u and John went on a wedding trip to the island of Hawai'i. Prince Lot Kapuāiwa, who became Kamehameha V, planned the trip and he and his retainers went along with them. Everywhere they went the Hawaiian people welcomed them warmly.

The couple lived with John's mother at Washington Place, a house built by John's father. This house is now owned by the state of Hawai'i and is the official home of Hawai'i's governor.

Waikīkī Estate

Although Liliʻu enjoyed living at Washington Place she never felt it was her own. In 1868 she inherited two houses in Waikīkī from her grandfather, ʻAikanaka, and she was so pleased she danced around the rooms. She wrote, "It was my own! Do you know what it means to have a place of your own?"

The houses were named Paoakalani, which means royal perfume, and Keʻalohilani, which means royal brightness. It was at Keʻalohilani that she spent much of her time composing her songs and translating Hawaiian stories into English.

Princess Lili'uokalani at home composing a song.

Lili'u always left her estate on the shore open for both Hawaiians and foreigners. Trees were planted for shade and fruits. Fishermen were able to launch their canoes there. Families spent the day there, bringing *poi* and bread and butter with them and buying fish from the fishermen.

Lili'u sometimes played her guitar and sang under the trees while her *hānai* daughter, Lydia Aholo, and her friends danced the *hula*. People enjoyed the entertainment so much that they threw money on the mats for the girls.

Princess Liliʻuokalani.
Photo courtesy of Bishop Museum

From Liliʻu to Liliʻuokalani

On April 11, 1877, Liliʻu's brother, King Kalākaua, declared her his heir apparent to the throne. Their brother, Leleiohoku, who had been heir apparent, had died the previous day.

It was on April 11 that Lili'u became known as Princess Lili'uokalani. Her name change was her brother's wish. Her first reaction to the name was that it was "no name at all...David chose it because it sounded more royal."

Lili'u preferred the name given her at birth and told her brother she did not want a name that was "not her own." Kalākaua told her if she did not accept it he would choose someone else to be heir apparent. Lili'u gave in and became known as Princess Lili'uokalani.

A Working Princess

Lili'uokalani took her role as princess seriously. She worked very hard to help her brother and her people. She felt a responsibility to be in touch with Hawaiians throughout the kingdom so in 1877 she visited all of the main islands.

One of her trips was to the leper colony on Moloka'i. She was the first *ali'i* to visit the colony. She showed her *aloha* for the lepers by taking gifts of cloth, food, pictures and feathers to them.

Upon her arrival Father Damien and eight hundred lepers welcomed her. Wheezing and straining, they sang for her. Seeing their misery and suffering, she decided to send medicines, books, music and furniture to the colony when she returned to Honolulu.

As a princess Lili'uokalani showed she could be a good leader. When Kalākaua went on a trip in 1881 he asked her to be regent while he was gone. He offered to appoint a regency council to help her, but she felt capable of doing the job alone. He then appointed her sole regent.

Shortly after Kalākaua left a smallpox epidemic broke out on O'ahu. Lili'uokalani asked the government ministers to stop travel between the islands in order to prevent the spread of the epidemic. Through her efforts the epidemic was confined to O'ahu.

When travel between the islands was again allowed, Lili'uokalani traveled to Hilo. Mauna Loa had been erupting for nine months, endangering Hilo residents.

Many Hawaiians believed the volcano goddess Pele was causing the eruption. They felt Pele might stop the eruptions if given offerings. Lili'uokalani's Christian beliefs told her otherwise. She ordered all churches opened for prayer meetings. She went to church to pray to God to stop the lava flow. Within a week the volcano ceased to erupt. She was convinced that her Christian God had succeeded over Pele.

Princess Liliʻuokalani and Queen Kapiʻolani (seated)
in England in 1887.

Photo courtesy of Bishop Museum

The Golden Jubilee

Lili'uokalani's duties as princess were not all work. In 1887 she was able to meet the royalty of England. King Kalākaua asked her to go with his wife, Kapi'olani, to the Golden Jubilee of Queen Victoria of England. As Kapi'olani spoke only Hawaiian, Lili'uokalani was to be her interpreter for the trip.

Princess Lili'uokalani and Queen Kapi'olani and group at
Stewart Estate, England in 1887.

Photo courtesy of Bishop Museum

The jubilee celebration was held in Westminster Abbey, the church where British monarchs are crowned. The royal gathering of kings and queens and princes and princesses from around the world impressed Lili'uokalani.

While Lili'uokalani was in England Kalākaua signed a new constitution for Hawai'i. It became known as the Constitution of 1887 or the Bayonet Constitution. It took from the monarch most of his power to make decisions and gave it to the cabinet and legislature, most of whom were not Hawaiian. Lili'uokalani was not happy with the new constitution.

Princess Lili'uokalani's "English Clock."

Photo by Kamehameha Schools

The English Clock

While going to and from England Lili'uokalani traveled through the United States. It was there that she acquired a clock which still hangs in one of Hawai'i's churches.

It was not an ordinary clock. Instead of numbers the clock had twelve letters, L-I-L-I-U-O-K-A-L-A-N-I. It told more than the time of the day. In three circles it marked the days of the week, the months and weeks of the year and the phases of the moon. Although the clock was made in America the Hawaiians called it "The English Clock."

This unusual clock was given to the members of a church in Waialua. The people of Waialua loved Lili'uokalani and, in time, their church became known as the Lili'uokalani Protestant Church.

A Sad Start

Lili'uokalani served as regent until January 29, 1891, the day King Kalākaua's body was returned from San Francisco. It was the first day of her reign but it was not a happy way to start.

Queen Lili'uokalani at 'Iolani Palace on the first day of her reign.

Photo courtesy of Bishop Museum

It began with her brother arriving home in a coffin. Lili'uokalani had no idea her brother had died in California. She was planning a celebration at 'Iolani Palace for him. When the ship carrying Kalākaua home arrived draped in black and with its flags at half mast, it was the first she knew of his death.

Grieving for her brother, Liliʻuokalani took the oath of office as queen and pledged to uphold the Constitution of 1887. This added to her unhappiness as she had disliked this constitution from the day her brother had accepted it.

Seven months later Lili'uokalani's husband John, whom she depended on for companionship and advice, died.

Through all this she did not give up. She continued striving toward a goal which led to one of the unhappiest events of her life.

The queen's book.
Photo by Kamehameha Schools

The Queen's Story

The queen's goal was to give Hawai'i a new constitution. In her book, *Hawaii's Story by Hawaii's Queen,* Lili'uokalani wrote she decided to write a new constitution because her ministers encouraged her to do so. Even more important, the Hawaiian people encouraged her to do so. She had received many petitions calling for a new constitution.

Her new constitution included two very important items. First, only male subjects, Hawaiian born or naturalized, could vote. Second, the monarch did not need to get the cabinet's approval for all government measures. In other words, the decision-making power of the monarch, which the Constitution of 1887 had taken away, was given back to the monarch.

The queen felt she had every right to write a new constitution as she was doing what her people wanted and as she was doing exactly what Kamehameha V had done in 1864. He had written a new constitution without even "asking a vote from anybody."

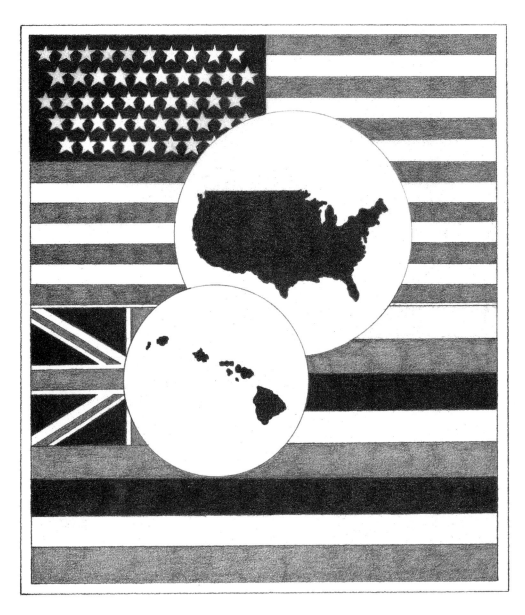

Annexation—the United States and Hawai'i together.

The Other Side of the Story

Queen Liliʻuokalani's views were not the same as those of several pro-American businessmen. These men asked themselves, "If the queen tries to change the Constitution of 1887 what should we do?"

Their answer was, "If the queen wants absolute control, we want annexation to the United States."

The Annexation Commission.
Photo courtesy of Hawai'i State Archives

Hawai'i's poor economic situation at that time increased the importance of annexation. The McKinley Tariff was largely responsible for the depressed business environment. It allowed all foreign sugar into the United States without being taxed. With this law Hawai'i had lost its earlier advantage over other countries.

The Reciprocity Treaty, which had allowed Hawaiian goods and American goods to be exchanged without tax, no longer mattered to the sugar business. Now all countries had this privilege with regard to sugar.

Further, sugar grown in the United States was given a two cent per pound price support. Pro-American businessmen decided annexation to the United States was the answer to protect their sugar profits.

The Committee of Safety.

Photo courtesy of Hawai'i State Archives

There was another business reason these men wanted annexation. A small number of men, mostly Americans, owned most of the private land and ran most of the businesses. They were afraid that as long as a Hawaiian monarch was in power what they owned could be taken away from them.

These men formed the Annexation Club, which later became the Committee of Safety.

To avoid trouble with the Committee of Safety the queen's ministers convinced her not to submit her new constitution. She was a peaceful woman and listened to them but it was already too late. The Committee of Safety had decided it was time to overthrow her.

United States Minister John L. Stevens.

Photo courtesy of Hawai'i State Archives

Why did the Hawaiian government allow the overthrow to happen? Why did Lili'uokalani allow herself to be overthrown?

In the many documents describing events which took place before the overthrow it appears the members of the Committee of Safety carried out their plans only when they were sure of American sympathy and support. United States Minister John Stevens was consulted before every important step taken to overthrow the queen. In the end, because of the American intervention, the overthrow was a fairly quiet affair.

Sanford B. Dole.
Photo courtesy of Hawai'i State Archives

While the queen's ministers were still trying to get US Minister Stevens to support her, Sanford Dole, the man chosen by the Committee of Safety to head the new government, was standing in front of Aliʻiōlani Hale, the government building, proclaiming Liliʻuokalani's kingdom and government no longer hers.

The Provisional Government established by the annexationists would be in charge until the Republic of Hawai'i was formed. Minister Stevens had told the Committee of Safety he would support the government in power. With that assurance the Committee of Safety then went and took over the government building.

When Sanford Dole went to take over the building, there was hardly anyone there. It was handed over by the head clerk of the Interior Department. Having taken control of the government offices the Provisional Government began the business of running Hawai'i.

And so it came to pass that Queen Lili'uokalani was overthrown on January 17, 1893.

Queen Liliʻuokalani at her desk writing her note of surrender to the United States.

The Queen Surrenders

Where was Lili'uokalani when all of this was going on? She was at home at 'Iolani Palace. When Sanford Dole made his speech she did not hear a word. Later she was to hear from her ministers that she was no longer ruler of Hawai'i.

What did Lili'uokalani do? She did not surrender to the Provisional Government. She surrendered to the United States of America. She did not give up absolutely and permanently. She gave up only temporarily and conditionally until the United States government studied the facts.

The Executive Council of the Provisional Government.

Photo courtesy of Bishop Museum

Annexation or No

With the queen's surrender the Provisional Government stayed in power. However, the main goal of that government was annexation to the United States. Five men were sent to Washington, D.C., to persuade US officials to annex Hawai'i.

United States Special Commissioner James H. Blount and his wife.

Photo courtesy of Hawai'i State Archives

President Grover Cleveland sent his own representative, Commissioner James Blount, to Hawai'i to investigate what had happened.

When Commissioner Blount arrived in March of 1893 he found the United States flag flying and United States troops on duty in downtown Honolulu. Mr. Blount ordered the American flags taken down and sent the troops back to their ship.

Commissioner Blount talked with Hawaiians and non-Hawaiians and drew his own conclusions.

This is what he told President Cleveland:
First, United States Minister John Stevens had helped non-Hawaiians in overthrowing the monarchy by sending United States Marines into town.
Second, the queen's overthrow was wrong and she should be given back her throne and kingdom.

After President Cleveland heard from Commissioner Blount he would not support the Provisional Government and would not support annexation of Hawai'i to the United States.

President Cleveland knew it was not the Hawaiian people who overthrew the queen but a small group of non-Hawaiians who were assisted by an armed force of United States Marines.

He felt that Minister Stevens should never have used the name and power of the United States to help the Committee of Safety. And President Cleveland would not support a government that had no support from the Hawaiian people.

A Major Obstacle

Why did Lili'uokalani not get her kingdom back if the president of the United States concluded the Provisional Government was wrong? The major obstacle was the United States Senate.

While the United States House of Representatives agreed with President Cleveland the senate did not.

Some senators worried about what the queen would do to those who had overthrown her. In other words, they were not sure what the queen would do with the pro-American businessmen if she regained power. The senate decided to have its own investigation.

According to Lili'uokalani the US Senate investigators only interviewed supporters of the Provisional Government. The senators concluded that the Provisional Government was probably right in overthrowing the queen when she tried to change the constitution.

Whether right or wrong, the Hawaiian monarchy had been overthrown. The men who had deposed the queen had earlier been recognized by President Benjamin Harrison, the president in office before President Cleveland. Since President Harrison had been sympathetic to the annexationists the United States Senate would not support President Cleveland.

With these mixed signals from Washington the Provisional Government proceeded on its way. It continued to send representatives to Washington to lobby for Hawai'i's annexation to the United States.

When annexation did not come quickly the Provisional Government proclaimed Hawai'i a republic. This occurred on July 4, 1894, a sad day for Lili'uokalani. The Republic of Hawai'i took possession of the government and the crown lands of Hawai'i.

Lili'uokalani and the Hawaiian people lost not only their government but their lands as well.

The Fight Goes On

The queen and her supporters did not give up easily. Her supporters continued to go to Washington to ask for the return of the monarchy. Unfortunately they failed to convince enough powerful individuals to support their cause.

Since talking had done no good some of Lili‘uokalani's supporters decided fighting with arms might work. Guns were brought in from San Francisco and hidden in the ground around Honolulu. Bombs were made and hidden as well.

One hiding place was in the queen's garden. Unfortunately for the queen and her supporters the government heard about these guns and bombs and several people were arrested before any attack was ever made.

The throne room of ʻIolani Palace where Queen Liliʻuokalani was tried and convicted.

Photo courtesy of Bishop Museum

Lili'uokalani's overthrow was not the last wrong she would suffer. On January 16, 1895, she was arrested at Washington Place. When her garden was searched bombs, rifles, pistols, cartridge belts, ammunition and swords were found.

The government accused her of trying to regain her throne, even though she said she was not aware of any plans to put her back in power. She was tried in the throne room of 'Iolani Palace and convicted.

Lili'uokalani was sentenced to pay a five thousand dollar fine and serve five years at hard labor.

Lili'uokalani did not pay the fine or spend five years in prison. Instead, she spent eight months in a corner room of what was then called the Executive Building, the renamed 'Iolani Palace.

In her words, "My home became my prison." In her writings of this time she had not one harsh word regarding her treatment. All the limitations imposed on her did not keep her from using her mind.

During this time she asked for paper and pencil to transcribe "Aloha 'Oe." She had composed it many years before. It is a song that is interpreted in different ways, but most agree it is a great love song. The following is a translation:

Aloha ʻOe

Proudly the rain on the cliffs
Creeps into the forest
Seeking the buds
And miniature *lehua* flowers of
the uplands.

Chorus

Farewell to you, farewell to you,
O fragrance in the blue depths
One fond embrace and I leave
To meet again.

Sweet memories come
Sound softly in my heart.
You are my beloved sweetheart
Felt within.

I understand the beauty
Of rose blossoms at Mauna-wili.
There the birds delight,
Alert the beauty of this flower.

Another song which Lili'uokalani worked on was "Ke Aloha O Ka Haku," otherwise known as "The Queen's Prayer." This song is still sung in many churches in Hawai'i today. She wrote the song for her niece, Ka'iulani, her heir apparent. One can only imagine how Lili'uokalani felt writing the following:

The Queen's Prayer

Your love
Is in heaven,
And your truth
So perfect.

I live in sorrow
Imprisoned,
You are my light,
Your glory my support.

Behold not with malevolence
The sins of man
But forgive
And cleanse.

And so, O Lord,
Beneath your wings
Be our peace
Forever more.

Queen Liliʻuokalani reading her crumpled newspaper.

Along with working on her songs Lili'uokalani did many other things to keep her spirits up. Although she was not officially allowed reading material she was able to read the newspapers wrapped around flowers sent by friends. She enjoyed playing her guitar and autoharp. She cared for her plants and crocheted. A canary brought her joy and companionship.

Although it was a far from easy task, Lili'uokalani showed she could survive her imprisonment.

A Hawaiian in America

When Lili'uokalani was released from prison she decided to take a trip. She wrote, "I felt greatly inclined to go abroad, it made no difference where, as long as it would be a change."

On December 5, 1896, she left Hawai'i and visited friends and her husband's relatives in San Francisco and Boston. "My husband's relatives made me feel I was not a stranger in a strange land."

In January of 1897 Liliʻuokalani left Boston for Washington, D.C., and met with President Cleveland. She wrote, "It was a pleasure for me to tell him how dear his name was to the Hawaiian people, and how grateful a place he held in my own heart because of his effort, to do that which was right and just in restoring to us our lost independence. We always thought him to be sincere in his attempt to right the wrong."

While in Washington she also finished translating the Hawaiian creation chant, *The Kumulipo.* It was a chant which had been handed down by her family from ancient times.

This was not to be her only trip to Washington. She made another trip when President McKinley sent his Annexation Treaty to the senate in June of 1897. She sent a protest to the treaty to the president but her effort was in vain. She made seven trips to the capital, none of which did her any good.

Queen Lili'uokalani seated in chair on the grounds of Washington Place.
Photo courtesy of Bishop Museum

The End of the Hawaiian Kingdom

After her imprisonment Liliʻuokalani returned to Washington Place. She was told to use the name Lydia Dominis but this did not stop people from calling her Liliʻuokalani. To the Hawaiian people she would always be their queen.

Did Liliʻuokalani fall apart and despair? No, what she did was write a book. In the spring and summer of 1897 she wrote her autobiography, *Hawaii's Story by Hawaii's Queen.* In this book she told of her story to preserve the kingdom of Hawaiʻi.

Prince David Kawananakoa, Princess Kaʻiulani, Queen Liliʻuokalani and friends at Washington Place while the annexation ceremony was taking place at the Executive Building (ʻIolani Palace).

Photo courtesy of Bishop Museum

The preservation of the Hawaiian kingdom was not to be. On July 7, 1898, President William McKinley signed a resolution annexing Hawai'i to the United States. Hawai'i was no longer Lili'uokalani's island kingdom.

When the annexation ceremony was held at the Executive Building Lili'uokalani, her niece Ka'iulani and their supporters remained at home.

Cannon salute for the annexation.
Photo courtesy of Bishop Museum

President Sanford B. Dole and United States Minister Harold M. Sewall tranferring
Hawai'i's sovereignty to the United States.

Photo courtesy of Bishop Museum,
Davey Collection

The Hawaiian flag being lowered at the Executive Building (ʻIolani Palace)
on August 12, 1898.

Photo courtesy of Bishop Museum,
Ray Jerome Baker Collection

American flags atop the Executive Building (ʻIolani Palace) on August 12, 1898.

Photo courtesy of Bishop Museum,
Davey Collection

"In front of the Executive Building there were Americans, Portuguese, Japanese, Chinese...
but no Hawaiians. The ceremonies had the tension of an execution."
Mabel Craft writing at the scene on Annexation Day.

Photo courtesy of Hawai'i State Archives

Two years later, on June 4, 1900, Hawai'i became a territory of the United States and Sanford Dole became its first governor. The annexationists had achieved their goal.

Lili'uokalani had lost. Though many sympathized with her, their sympathy did not bring back the Hawaiian kingdom.

Princess Kalaniana'ole, Queen Lili'uokalani and Mrs. George Smithers (Maili).

Photo courtesy of Bishop Museum

The Queen's Legacy

Lili'uokalani had a wealth of *aloha* all of her life, but she did not have a wealth of money in her later years. She was never given just compensation for the crown lands which were taken from her.

By her estimation the crown lands included 911,888 acres and were worth twenty million dollars. She asked for ten million dollars in compensation but received nothing.

She still had Washington Place as well as homes in Kāhala, Pālama, Wai'alae, Waialua and Waikīkī. She also had a modest income. It was not until 1912 that the Territory of Hawai'i began paying her twelve thousand dollars a year.

Queen Lili'uokalani at home on March 10, 1913.

Photo courtesy of Bishop Museum,
Edgeworth Collection

It is said that Lili'uokalani had large pockets sewn into her clothing so she could fill them with candy to give to children. Although she had no children of her own, she had three *hānai* children whom she loved dearly: John Aimoku Dominis, Kaiponohea Aea and Lydia Aholo Dominis. Her love for children survives to this day—for in 1909 she established a trust for Hawaiian children in need which continues to aid those for whom she cared so much.

Queen Liliʻuokalani with four young girls, possibly in Kona, ca. 1915.
Photo courtesy of Bishop Museum

Today the Queen Lili'uokalani Children's Center provides counseling and guidance to Hawaiian families on the islands of O'ahu, Hawai'i, Maui, Kaua'i and Moloka'i. It provides help to some twenty-six hundred children a year. The trust's income comes from land holdings. Like her sister Bernice Pauahi Bishop, Lili'uokalani left her estate for the well-being of Hawai'i's children.

Queen Liliʻuokalani lying in state at Kawaiahaʻo Church, November 1917.
Photo courtesy of Bishop Museum

Aloha 'Oe

On the day Lili'uokalani died, November 11, 1917, church bells were rung throughout Honolulu. She had lived her life as a deposed queen in a quiet and dignified manner. When the end came her people remained loyal to her and came to bid her *"aloha."*

Those who love her still visit her today at Mauna'ala, the Royal Mausoleum in Nu'uanu.

Conclusion

Lili'uokalani said her name was "no name at all," and perhaps her name was a forecast of what was to come... where she ended with "no kingdom at all."

Her story shows how perceptive Kamehameha III was when he started the Chiefs' Children's School. His reasons were to have the *ali'i* children learn English and to have them deal effectively with foreigners. As fluent in English and intelligent a woman as Lili'uokalani was, her interactions with foreigners were still not effective in preserving her kingdom.

Foreign influence began long before she was born and continued throughout the monarchy period and beyond.

More than a century after Queen Liliʻuokalani's overthrow, we are still reminded of the stalwart queen who did what she thought was right and was dethroned for what others thought was wrong.

Bibliography

Allen, Helena G. *The Betrayal of Lili'uokalani.* Glendale, Ca.: The Arthur H. Clark Co., 1982.

Apple, Russ, and Peg Apple. *Land, Lili'uokalani and Annexation.* Honolulu: Topgallant Publishing Co., 1979.

Boggs, Stephen. "The Overthrow of the Hawaiian Monarchy." Paper preceding the Kamehameha Secondary School Faculty Program Committee Lecture, Honolulu, September 14, 1992.

Cooke, Amos Starr, and Juliette Montague Cooke. *The Hawaiian Chiefs' Children's School.* Rutland, Vt.: Charles E. Tuttle Co., 1970.

Dudley, Michael Kioni, and Keoni Kealoha Agard. *A Call for Hawaiian Sovereignty.* Honolulu: Nā Kāne o Ka Malo Press, 1990.

Hodges, William C., Jr. *The Passing of Liliuokalani, Preceded by A Brief Historical Interpretation of the Life of Liliuokalani of Hawaii.* Honolulu: Honolulu Star-Bulletin Publishers, 1918.

Irwin, Bernice Piilani. *I Knew Queen Liliuokalani.* Honolulu: South Seas Sales, 1960.

Joesting, Edward. *Hawaii: An Uncommon History.* New York: W.W. Norton & Company, 1972.

Kuykendall, Ralph S. *The Hawaiian Kingdom,* Vol. 3. Honolulu: University of Hawaii Press, 1967.

Kuykendall, Ralph S., and A. Grove Day. *Hawaii: A History.* Englewood Cliffs, N.J.: Prentice-Hall, Inc., 1976.

Lau, Rodney Kalani. "Lili'uokalani, Memories of Lydia Aholo." Honolulu, 1968.

Liliuokalani. *Hawaii's Story By Hawaii's Queen.* Tokyo: Charles E. Tuttle Co., 1964.

Lucas, Clorinda. "Queen Lili'uokalani," Mother's Day Sermon at the Bishop Memorial Chapel. Honolulu, 1968.

Oleson, David L. "Aloha Oe, Liliuokalani!," letter written to a friend. Honolulu, 1917. Hawaiian Collection, Midkiff Learning Center, Kamehameha Schools, Honolulu.

Seiden, Alan. *Hawai'i: The Royal Legacy.* Honolulu: Mutual Publishing, 1992.

Warriner, Emily V. *A Royal Journey to London.* Honolulu: Topgallant Publishing Co., 1975.

KAMEHAMEHA SCHOOLS

Kamehameha Schools Press, the publishing arm of Kamehameha Schools, traces its roots to the schools' very beginning. In the schools' early years students learned printing as a craft, producing newspapers and manuals.

Kamehameha Schools was founded by Princess Bernice Pauahi Bishop, great-granddaughter and last royal descendant of the Hawaiian ruler Kamehameha I. Her will established Kamehameha Schools to educate Hawaiian children. With over five thousand students in kindergarten through twelfth grade it is the largest independent school system in the United States.

Kamehameha School for Boys was first established, in 1887, on what are now the grounds of the Bishop Museum. A year later the Preparatory Department, for boys six to twelve, opened in adjacent facilities. The School for Girls opened nearby in 1894 on its own campus *ma kai* of King Street. Between 1930 and 1955 all three schools moved to the current six-hundred-acre hillside campus on Kapālama Heights.

The first book identified as a Kamehameha Schools Press publication, *Ancient Hawaiian Civilization,* was published in 1933. Following this publication many other classic books on Hawai'i have been produced. In-house printing ended in the 1970s when Kamehameha's curriculum shifted from vocational to college preparatory.

Kamehameha Schools Press now issues reference books on Hawaiian history, adult- and student-level biographies of key figures in Hawaiian history, collections of Hawaiian folklore, and curriculum materials for the teaching of Hawaiian history and studies at various grade levels. One of the press' efforts is publishing in Hawaiian language, including historical materials and the issuing of biographical and other titles in modern Hawaiian translations, supporting and leading in the contemporary revitalization of Hawaiian as a living spoken language.

http://kspress.ksbe.edu/